OVERCOMING ADVERSITY:
SHARING THE AMERICAN DREAM

MALCOLM X

MASON CREST PUBLISHERS

OVERCOMING ADVERSITY:
SHARING THE AMERICAN DREAM

Charles Barkley

Halle Berry

Cesar Chavez

Kenny Chesney

George Clooney

Johnny Depp

Tony Dungy

Jermaine Dupri

Jennifer Garner

Kevin Garnett

John B. Herrington

Salma Hayek

Vanessa Hudgens

Samuel L. Jackson

Norah Jones

Martin Lawrence

Bruce Lee

Eva Longoria

Malcolm X

Carlos Mencia

Chuck Norris

Barack Obama

Rosa Parks

Bill Richardson

Russell Simmons

Carrie Underwood

Modern American

Indian Leaders

OVERCOMING ADVERSITY:
SHARING THE AMERICAN DREAM

MALCOLM X

CAMMY S. BOURCIER

MASON CREST PUBLISHERS
PHILADELPHIA

ABOUT CROSS-CURRENTS

When you see this logo, turn to the Cross-Currents section at the back of the book. The Cross-Currents features explore connections between people, places, events, and ideas.

Produced by OTTN Publishing, Stockton, New Jersey

Mason Crest Publishers
370 Reed Road
Broomall, PA 19008
www.masoncrest.com

First printing

1 3 5 7 9 8 6 4 2

Library of Congress Cataloging-in-Publication Data

Bourcier, Cammy S.
  Malcolm X / by Cammy S. Bourcier.
      p. cm. — (Sharing the American dream)
  Includes bibliographical references (p.   ).
  ISBN 978-1-4222-0577-8 (hc) — ISBN 978-1-4222-0755-0 (pb)
  1. X, Malcolm, 1925-1965—Juvenile literature. 2. African American
Muslims—Biography—Juvenile literature. I. Title.
  BP223.Z8L57196 2008
  320.54'6092—dc22
  [B]
                              2008023435

OVERCOMING ADVERSITY:
SHARING THE AMERICAN DREAM

TABLE OF CONTENTS

CHAPTER ONE

FREEDOM BEHIND BARS

It was February 1946. Malcolm Little had not yet reached his 21st birthday. He hadn't even started shaving. But here he was, locked up in Charleston State Prison in Massachusetts, facing a sentence of up to 10 years behind bars for a burglary.

Malcolm Little was a very angry young man. He couldn't get the illegal drugs he craved. His cell was cramped and dirty, with only a covered pail for a toilet. And he had no reason for hope and virtually nothing to believe in.

For years, he had thought like an animal, with great instincts for survival. But now he was caged, pacing like a leopard, and there were no signs that he was going to be tamed quickly.

Fellow inmates called him Satan because of his disrespect for religion. He was also nasty to everyone. He cursed at the guards and raged at psychologists.

The Power of Words

One of the first men to gain Malcolm's trust in jail was an old-time burglar he called Bimbi in his autobiography. What impressed Malcolm most about Bimbi was that when he talked, everyone listened. In his autobiography, Malcolm wrote, "He was the first man I had ever seen command total respect . . . with his words."

Malcolm X, 1964. Malcolm rose from poverty and a life of petty crime to become one of the most influential champions of African American empowerment and civil rights.

Bimbi talked Malcolm into using his spare time to take advantage of the prison courses and the library. That was Malcolm's first step toward freedom.

Malcolm's vocabulary at the time, he admitted, was limited to about 200 words. Determined, he spent hundreds of hours copying words from the dictionary and learning what they meant. "Months passed without my even thinking about being imprisoned. In fact, up to then, I never had been so truly free in my life."

Malcolm devoured books on all sorts of topics, but especially philosophy and history. He said, in his autobiography, that he read as much as 15 hours a day, often by a dim light, learning the beliefs of some of humanity's greatest thinkers. "The ability to read awoke inside me some long dormant craving to be mentally alive," he later recalled.

Through his reading, Malcolm also came to understand the full horror of slavery, which he called the "world's most monstrous crime." He developed a new respect for Africa and its historical greatness. It was not long before he was sharing his views with the other black prisoners, many of whom had never thought about the horrible lives their ancestors had endured as slaves.

Seeing the Light

Malcolm was transferred to Concord Reformatory in January 1947. The following year, he received a letter from his brother Philbert, who wrote to Malcolm about his discovery of the "natural religion" for black people and a new organization he had joined. It was called the Nation of Islam. At first Malcolm wanted nothing to do with the Nation of Islam. But then his brother Reginald wrote and told him that if he stopped smoking and eating pork—both of which were forbidden by the Nation of Islam—he would get out of jail.

Malcolm didn't really believe this. But, figuring he had nothing to lose, he decided to follow Reginald's advice. Besides, it made him proud to stand out among his fellow prisoners for being different.

For some time, Malcolm had wanted desperately to be transferred to the experimental prison colony at Norfolk, Massachusetts. That institution had been described to him as a place that was as close to paradise as any prison could be. In 1947, Malcolm had sent a letter to prison authorities requesting a transfer to Norfolk. In late 1948, partly through the efforts of his older half sister Ella Little Collins, he got the transfer.

His life in prison took a very positive turn. There was more freedom and fresh air at Norfolk. There were group discussions and visiting instructors from nearby universities. There were books he could read aimlessly in the library. He joined the debating team.

READ MORE

The Norfolk Prison Colony, where Malcolm served part of his sentence, was designed as a model prison community where inmates would be rehabilitated before their return to society. For details, see page 44.

Elijah Muhammad

It was during this period that Malcolm learned, from his family, about Elijah Muhammad. Muhammad was the leader of the Nation of Islam, a religious organization that had been established in Detroit during the 1930s. The Nation of Islam took its name from—and shared certain beliefs with—the religion of Islam, which was founded in the seventh century A.D. by the prophet Muhammad. But some of what the Nation of Islam taught was in direct conflict with the beliefs of Muslims (as followers of Islam are called). For example, Muslims believe that

Allah (or God) has spoken to humankind through a succession of prophets, the last and greatest of whom was Muhammad, who died in A.D. 632. Followers of the Nation of Islam, by contrast, said Elijah Muhammad was a prophet of God.

The Nation of Islam also had a racial orientation not present in mainstream Islam. The Nation taught that all people had originally been black. They had created great civilizations, with the center of the world being in Mecca (which is also the holiest city in mainstream Islam). Some 4,000 years ago, however, an evil scientist exiled from Mecca created the white race. Since that time, the "white devils" had kidnapped, enslaved, and brainwashed black people, removing accounts of their former achievements from the history books. Throughout this process, Christianity had been a tool whites had used to keep black people oppressed.

READ MORE

Worldwide, Islam has more than a billion followers. For some basic information on this religion, turn to page 45.

Malcolm Little's family encouraged him to write to Elijah Muhammad. He too had been in jail in earlier years and would understand what Malcolm was going through. Malcolm wrote to the Nation of Islam leader, and Elijah Muhammad wrote back. He told Malcolm that the black prisoner symbolized white society's crime of keeping black men oppressed, deprived, and ignorant, incapable of getting decent jobs and forcing them into a life of crime.

Elijah Muhammad's teachings made perfect sense to Malcolm. Whites wanted to keep blacks down. They wanted to make sure that they remained financially better off than blacks. They wanted to keep blacks from having any pride.

Malcolm studied the teachings of the Nation of Islam. He began to pray. While still in jail, he found Allah and decided to

Elijah Muhammad addresses his followers, 1964. Years earlier, the Nation of Islam leader had answered a letter from a young prisoner named Malcolm Little—a response that helped put Malcolm on the path to conversion.

become a member of the Nation of Islam. It completely transformed his life.

Free at Last

Malcolm was eventually kicked out of Norfolk Prison Colony because he was becoming too influential among the other inmates and causing trouble with his antiwhite views. He was returned to Charleston State Prison, where he served another year quietly. The day before he was released in August 1952, his sister Hilda gave him a small amount of money, a lecture, and a cheap suit. After six and a half years in jail, Malcolm Little was free.

CHAPTER TWO

SEEDS OF HATRED

The man who would become known as Malcolm X was born Malcolm Little on May 19, 1925, in Omaha, Nebraska. He was the fourth child of Earl Little, an outspoken Baptist minister, and his second wife, Louise.

Malcolm's parents came from very different backgrounds. Earl Little, born in Georgia in 1890, had received only a few years of formal education. Louise Norton Little, by contrast, was well educated. She was born on the island of Grenada in the British West Indies in 1897, the illegitimate daughter of a white man and a black woman. It was from her that Malcolm inherited his lighter complexion and his red hair.

Earl Little's life was shaped largely by the terrible racism that existed during the time. Not only were blacks denied the same rights as white people in many parts of the country, they were frequently the targets of racially motivated violence. Earl's three brothers were killed by whites.

So in addition to his work as a Baptist minister, Earl Little became a dedicated organizer for Marcus Garvey's Universal

READ MORE

For a profile of Marcus Garvey, founder of the Universal Negro Improvement Association, see page 46.

Marcus Garvey in 1924. Malcolm's parents, Earl and Louise Little, were members of Garvey's Universal Negro Improvement Association.

Negro Improvement Association (U.N.I.A.). The mission of U.N.I.A. was to convince black Americans to return to Africa, because, according to Garvey, they could never achieve freedom, independence, and self-respect in the United States. This belief made Garvey very controversial. It also made Earl Little very unpopular among the important white people in Omaha, where Earl and Louise had settled in 1923.

Violent Impressions

One of the first stories Malcolm would remember his mother telling him concerned an event that had occurred shortly before his birth. Earl was away, preaching in Milwaukee, Wisconsin, when hooded Ku Klux Klan riders came to the Little home. The KKK was a shadowy organization that terrorized—and often murdered—black people. Louise, pregnant and alone with her three small children, explained that her husband wasn't home. The KKK men warned her to tell Earl to quit spreading trouble among the "good Negroes" of Omaha with the "back to Africa" preaching of Marcus Garvey. Then they left, but not before they had shattered every windowpane in the Little home.

The Little family moved from Omaha shortly after Malcolm was born. They went first to Milwaukee, then settled in Lansing, Michigan, where Earl was hoping to start his own business. He was harassed almost immediately. A local hate group called "the Black Legion" accused him of spreading unrest among area blacks with his "uppity" ambitions. But they didn't limit their dislike of Earl to words alone.

Members of the Ku Klux Klan, circa 1922. The KKK, which was most powerful in the South, targeted blacks who refused to accept an inferior place in society.

One of Malcolm's earliest memories would concern an incident that happened shortly after the birth of his youngest sister, Yvonne. Malcolm was in bed when he was suddenly "snatched awake into a frightening confusion of pistol shots and shouting and smoke and flames." Two men had set fire to the Littles' house. Earl shot at them as they ran away, while Louise managed to hustle her children into the yard just before the house crashed in. "I remember we were outside in the night in our underwear, crying and yelling our heads off," Malcolm wrote in his autobiography. "The white police and firemen came and stood around watching as the house burned down to the ground."

Family Life

The home that Malcolm would remember best was situated two miles outside of Lansing. Earl Little built the house himself. Malcolm also recalled frequent visits from the police, who were suspicious of Earl's preaching activities.

If racial turmoil constantly threatened the Littles from without, major frictions existed within the family as well. Earl and Louise often did not get along. Malcolm thought this was due to Earl's resentment of his wife's education. Earl became very irritated whenever it appeared that Louise might be correcting him in any way. On occasion, he beat his wife, according to Malcolm. He also beat the older kids "almost savagely" for breaking any of his many rules. Malcolm himself was spared a lot of the violence from his father. He thought this was because he was the lightest-skinned of the children.

Economic concerns may also have contributed to the tensions within the Little household. By the early 1930s, the United States was mired in the Great Depression, a severe economic collapse. Many people were without homes and jobs, sleeping on the streets and starving. And it was hardest of all for blacks.

The Littles survived by raising much of their own food and living off the collections Earl got from preaching. Malcolm tended to a small garden. In it he loved growing peas and daydreaming.

Early Impressions

When Earl Little preached, Malcolm frequently accompanied him. Malcolm later wrote that he was confused by the jumping, shouting, singing, and praying. "I just couldn't believe in the Christian concept of Jesus as someone divine. . . . I had very little respect for most people who represented religion."

But Malcolm was proud of his father when he went with him to U.N.I.A. meetings. Sometimes as many as 20 people—all of them black—gathered in a living room. Often they were the same people Malcolm had seen jumping and singing in church. But here, they listened quietly as Earl crusaded for Marcus Garvey's cause. Malcolm didn't understand much of what his father said, but he had already experienced the racism of American society. The U.N.I.A. meetings always ended with his father leading his audience in chants: "Up you mighty race, you can accomplish what you will!"

Tragedy

On the evening of September 28, 1931, Earl and Louise Little had one of their bitter fights. Earl stormed angrily out of the house. Louise put the kids to bed, but they awoke several hours later to the sound of her screaming. Police were there with bad news: Earl, they said, had been killed after being run over by a streetcar. However, because Earl's skull was caved in on one side, there were doubts about the official story. "Negroes in Lansing," Malcolm later wrote, "have always whispered that he was attacked, and then laid across some tracks for a streetcar to run him over. His body was cut almost in half."

Louise Little did everything she could to keep her family together after Earl's death, but she faced huge obstacles. A company that had sold Earl a life insurance policy refused to pay Louise, saying that her husband had committed suicide. She was forced to accept charity even though she was a very proud woman who hated the idea of taking anything from others.

But what she hated even worse, according to Malcolm, were the officials from the state's welfare service, who came to the house often to check up on the family. "They acted and looked at her, and at us, and around in our house, in a way that had about it the feeling—at least for me—that we were not people," Malcolm would write. "In their eyesight we were just things, that was all." Whatever pride was left in the Little household began to evaporate.

By 1934, Malcolm had started drifting after school, stealing an apple here and there, staying away from home because he couldn't stand what was going on there. Eventually he got caught stealing, and state social workers took him out of the Little home. They placed him with another black family in the neighborhood. He thrived there for a while. But then the social workers delivered a major blow: convinced that Louise was mentally ill, they had her committed to the state mental hospital at Kalamazoo.

It was not long afterward that Malcolm got in trouble at Lansing West Junior High School for putting a thumbtack on a teacher's chair. He was off to a detention home in Mason, Michigan, about 12 miles away.

Time Out

The woman in charge of the detention home was Mrs. Swerlin. Malcolm recalled that she and her husband, who were white, treated him well. Still, they didn't think twice about saying bad things about other blacks. Malcolm did his chores around the house. On weekends he went to the black section of Lansing, where he hung around bars and restaurants and enjoyed listening to the big bands.

When Malcolm entered the seventh grade at Mason Junior High School, he was the only black student in the class. Nevertheless, he was very popular. Because he had the support of Mrs. Swerlin, who was highly respected, his classmates were eager to have him join their activities. These ranged from debating to playing basketball. Malcolm also got a job at a local restaurant as a dishwasher. He liked the feeling of getting paid every Friday night. In the second semester of his seventh-grade year, Malcolm's grades were the highest in the class, and he was also elected class president.

Ella Little Collins, Malcolm's half sister, speaks at a 1965 news conference. Malcolm, who lived with Ella during some of his teen years, would later call her "the first really proud black woman" he'd ever known.

Ella

Toward the end of seventh grade, Malcolm met Ella Little Collins, his grown half sister. She was the daughter of Earl Little and his first wife, Daisy Mason. The first of three children from that marriage, Ella left her home state of Georgia before she was 18 to earn a living in New York. A short time later, she moved to the Boston area, where she started making enough money to help her relatives who were still in the South.

When Malcolm met Ella for the first time, he described her as "the first really proud black woman I had ever seen in my life." He'd never been so impressed with anyone.

Ella was impressed with him, too. She found him lovable, smart, and curious and invited him to visit her in Roxbury, Massachusetts, that summer. He did, and although he returned to Michigan to finish the eighth grade, his life would never be the same.

CHAPTER THREE

LESSONS FROM THE STREET

Ella Little Collins was one of the first people in Malcolm's life to make him feel proud of his family. She told him all about his relatives, in Georgia and in Roxbury, a suburb of Boston where she now lived. He was all too happy to board a Greyhound bus during the summer of 1940 to meet members of his extended family.

His eyes were opened wide in Roxbury. Ella, who had by then made a significant amount of money through her business skills, was an important person in local black society. Malcolm was impressed. Also, he had never seen as many blacks as he did in downtown Roxbury at night. He was astonished by the nightclubs they went to, the down-home cooking they ate, and the cars they drove. The black churches he attended were finer than the white churches he knew in Mason, Michigan. By the time he returned home for the eighth grade, he was restless.

One Hope Dashed

A major turning point in Malcolm's life occurred when a favorite teacher gave him some jarring advice. Mr. Ostrowski, who had given him top grades in English, asked Malcolm what he wanted to do with his life. When Malcolm told him he was thinking

A view of Boston during the 1940s. The city and its suburbs were home to active and prosperous African American communities—something Malcolm had never seen before moving to the Boston area in 1941.

about becoming a lawyer, Ostrowski replied, "Malcolm, one of life's first needs is for us to be realistic. Don't misunderstand me, now. We all here like you, you know that. But you've got to be realistic about being [black]. A lawyer—that's no realistic goal."

Malcolm knew he was smart and didn't understand why he couldn't become what he wanted to be. He began drawing away from white people altogether. No one could understand what had come over him. He wanted to live in Roxbury with Ella, and the week that he finished eighth grade, he boarded the bus for Boston again. In his autobiography, Malcolm wrote, "All praise is due to Allah that I went to Boston when I did. If I hadn't, I'd probably still be a brainwashed black Christian."

Life in Roxbury

Ella's goal, her son Rodnell P. Collins wrote in *Seventh Child: A Family Memoir of Malcolm X*, was to provide Malcolm with a loving, secure, and structured environment where he could develop his potential. Ella recognized Malcolm's intellectual gifts and expected him to become a lawyer. What she didn't anticipate was how tempted he would be by street life in Roxbury.

Ella encouraged Malcolm to check out the town and get to know where the upper-class black people lived and socialized. But the youth was more drawn to the poorer section, with its cheap restaurants and bars. It wasn't long after he arrived in Roxbury that Malcolm began sneaking out of the house to go to the pool hall or charm his way into an after-hours club. In his book, Collins wrote that "despite our efforts, Malcolm was not to escape that trap that this society sets for too many young black males."

His first new friend was Malcolm "Shorty" Jarvis, a saxophone player. Shorty got Malcolm his first job, or "hustle": shining shoes at the Roseland State Ballroom in Boston. Ella wasn't happy, but Malcolm was overjoyed. Musicians, he wrote back home to Michigan, had never had a greater shoeshine-boy fan. It was at Roseland that Malcolm first smoked, drank, and gambled.

Zoot Suits and Conks

Malcolm was doing his best to act and look cool. Toward that end, he bought his first zoot suit. The outlandish outfit consisted of sky blue pants and a long, shoulder-padded coat. Malcolm completed his ensemble with a blue hat that had a feather in its big brim, in addition to a long, gold-plated chain.

He also got his hair straightened, or "conked." The word *conk* came from "congolene," the strong chemical that was used to flatten out black people's naturally curly hair. Conking was usually done at barbershops, but Shorty created a less expensive home version using a can of lye (a strong solution used to make soaps), white potatoes, and eggs. He warned Malcolm that the experience would not be pleasant. "You know it's going to burn when I comb it in—it burns bad—but the longer you can stand it, the straighter the hair." Malcolm wrote that his eyes watered and his nose ran. He cursed Shorty and told him he couldn't stand it any more. Finally came the rinse, with Shorty's assurance that he had taken it all rather well. "You got a good conk," Shorty said.

Later, Malcolm would recall that the conk was really his first big step toward self-degradation. He'd been brainwashed into

Dancers in zoot suits entertain patrons of a black nightclub, circa 1944. (Inset) An African American man gets his hair "conked."

believing that black people were inferior, and they had to hurt themselves to try to look handsome by white standards.

New Women in Malcolm's Life

Sporting his sharp new look, Malcolm took to clubs and parties, where he taught himself to dance. "I had always feared that dancing involved a certain order or pattern of specific steps—as dancing is done by whites," he wrote in his autobiography. But, high on marijuana and liquor, he discovered that it was simply a matter of letting your feet, hands, and body respond to the music.

He soon quit his job at the Roseland State Ballroom so he could spend his nights dancing. Ella stepped in again and got him a job as a soda jerk (a person who poured soft drinks) at the Townsend Drug Store near her home. There, Malcolm met a young black woman named Laura. She was a bookworm and an honors student, but she loved to dance. After finding out that Malcolm shared this passion, Laura started accompanying him to parties and clubs. The two of them always wowed the crowds with their dancing.

One night when he and Laura were dancing at Roseland, Malcolm found himself face to face with a blonde girl who had her eyes on him. In his autobiography, he calls her "Sophia." She was a good enough dancer, but that wasn't the attraction. What mattered to Malcolm was that she was beautiful and white. They became romantically involved almost immediately.

Harlem Days

When she learned about Malcolm's relationship with Sophia, Ella was outraged. But there seemed to be little she could do. Finally, through a friend of hers, Ella managed to get Malcolm a railroad job on the New Haven Yankee Clipper line. This would take him out of the area frequently—and maybe get him away from Sophia.

Eventually, Malcolm was assigned to work on the Boston–to–New York train run. He was thrilled: he would have a chance to visit Harlem, which was a famous center of black culture. Malcolm ultimately got fired from his railroad job because of complaints about his nasty attitude.

But he soon landed another job, as a waiter at a Harlem bar called Small's Paradise. It was 1942, and Malcolm was 17 years old.

READ MORE

During the 1920s and 1930s, Harlem flourished as a center of African American art, music, and culture. To learn more about this section of New York City, see page 47.

Harlem had been a hub for black artists, musicians, and writers. But it also had a seamy underside of con games, gambling, dope selling, and prostitution. It didn't take long for Malcolm to

Harlem street scene, 1942. The New York City neighborhood was famous for the vibrancy of its African American community.

get heavily involved in petty crime. When the New York City police got close to catching him, he began making runs on the rail lines again, following the big bands he loved.

By this time, the United States had entered World War II. Malcolm received a draft notice, but he managed to stay out of the army by pretending he was crazy: He told the army psychiatrist that he wanted to be sent to the South so he could organize blacks to shoot whites.

In New York, Malcolm pulled his first robbery. His life became a cycle of crime and drug abuse. He was high almost all the time. After Malcolm ran afoul of a well-known mobster, his old friend Shorty got him out of New York.

Return to Roxbury

Back in Roxbury, Malcolm got involved with Shorty in a burglary operation. They rented an apartment at Harvard Square and enlisted Sophia and her sister. The white girls would go to expensive homes and pretend to be selling something. If they were invited inside a home, the girls would look for valuable items. Later they would report back to Malcolm and Shorty, who would then burglarize the house. They stored the stolen goods in the Harvard Square apartment until the goods could be sold.

Shorty and Malcolm pulled off numerous burglaries. They finally got caught when Malcolm took an expensive watch he had stolen to a jeweler to be repaired. The jeweler had been alerted, and he contacted the police. When the police searched the Harvard Square apartment, they found loads of stolen goods.

Sophia and her sister claimed they had been forced into the criminal activity. They both received short jail sentences. Shorty and Malcolm, however, got 8 to 10 years in prison. Malcolm didn't really think he'd done anything wrong.

CHAPTER FOUR

GROWING A NATION

When he left prison in the summer of 1952, Malcolm headed straight to Detroit, Michigan. This was largely at the urging of his family. They wanted him away from the temptations of Harlem and Roxbury. They also wanted him to become a member of a Nation of Islam temple.

Malcolm's brother Wilfred got him a job at a furniture store. The store lured poor blacks in with the promise of "no money down" bargains. What the customers didn't realize was that they would be paying almost criminally high interest rates. For the first time, Malcolm saw how whites enriched themselves by robbing black people like him.

A Muslim Life

At Wilfred's home, Malcolm joined in the routines and rituals that Muslims all over the world perform each day. After rising, he, Wilfred, and Wilfred's family would perform the ritual washings to prepare themselves for morning prayers—the first of five times Muslims pray each day. They would gather on a prayer rug and face east, toward the holy city of Mecca to pray to Allah.

During this period, Malcolm started attending Temple Number One. Located in Detroit, it was the first Nation of Islam

Malcolm's magnetic personality—along with his keen intellect and devotion to Elijah Muhammad—helped make him a rising star in the Nation of Islam by the mid-1950s.

temple to be established. Malcolm was enchanted by the dress and manner of the men, women, and children. It was like nothing he'd ever seen in the Christian churches. But he couldn't believe there were so many empty seats. That was when he realized that he could play a huge role in the growth of the Nation of Islam.

In September 1952, he got a big opportunity when he met Elijah Muhammad for the first time at Temple Number Two in Chicago. Malcolm said he was electrified when he heard the Nation of Islam leader speak. After preaching, Muhammad spoke directly to Malcolm. He warned Malcolm that it would be more difficult to follow the rules of Islam outside of jail because of the temptations. Malcolm was not concerned. Instead, he told Muhammad that he was committed to recruiting more members to join the Nation. Muhammad told him to "fish" for the young people first, since they were the ones most likely to fall into the path of sin.

Back in Detroit, Malcolm led a recruitment drive. It was at this time that his request to formally change his name was granted. He gave up what he called his "slave name" and became Malcolm X.

READ MORE

For information on the significance of Malcolm X's adopted last name, see page 48.

Fishing Big Time

Malcolm left his job at the furniture store and got a new one at the Ford Motor Company's Lincoln-Mercury assembly line. He had already been named assistant minister at Detroit's Temple Number One and was busy "fishing" young black men from the streets. He tried to save them from lives of crime and alcohol and drug abuse. He dramatized the horror of slavery for them whenever he could.

Malcolm left his job at Ford to dedicate himself fully to his religious work. He studied and became more immersed in worship rituals. Soon, he was asked to open Temple Number Eleven in Boston. In March 1954, he went to Philadelphia, where he opened Temple Number Twelve three months later. Then came the best appointment of them all: he was appointed minister of Temple Number Seven in Harlem. The temple was a modest

In 1954 Malcolm X was appointed minister of Temple Number Seven in Harlem, where he worked hard to win converts. Here Malcolm talks to a woman inside a Nation of Islam restaurant.

storefront, but New York City had more than a million black people Malcolm might be able to convert.

There was resistance to the Nation of Islam's message. Many people did not like the strict moral code and discipline of the Nation of Islam community. Temple Seven grew, but slowly. Elijah Muhammad told Malcolm to be patient.

Malcolm Finds a Wife

Malcolm was so busy growing the Nation that he had no time for romance. His previous relationships had also left him distrustful of women.

Then he met Betty Sanders. Sister Betty X had joined the Nation of Islam in 1956. She had attended college and was now in nursing school. Malcolm, who by that time was the Nation of Islam's most eligible bachelor, was under pressure to find a wife.

One day, he offered to take Betty to the Museum of Natural History in New York, to show her some exhibits that supported Elijah Muhammad's teachings.

Later, Malcolm suggested that she attend a women's class at the Nation of Islam's Headquarters Temple Two in Chicago. In fact, he wanted Elijah Muhammad's blessing for him to marry Betty. The Nation of Islam leader approved.

Sister Betty X—formerly Betty Sanders—joined Temple Seven in 1956. Less than two years later, she and Malcolm X were married.

Malcolm and Betty were married in Lansing on January 14, 1958. Together, they had six daughters. In his autobiography, Malcolm said, "Betty was the only woman I ever thought about loving."

Competing Strategies for Black Rights

Although Malcolm was anxious about what he perceived as the slow growth of the Nation of Islam, membership was increasing as the activities of the organization were getting more attention from the media. Secretly, the Nation was also getting a lot of attention from other sources: the Federal Bureau of Investigation (FBI) and the Central Intelligence Agency (CIA). Officials in the FBI and CIA suspected the Nation of "anti-white"—and anti-American—activities.

During the late 1950s and 1960s, the mainstream civil rights movement—led by people such as Martin Luther King Jr.—sought to ensure that black Americans had the same legal rights and the same opportunities as white Americans. The way to accomplish this, the civil rights leaders believed, was through the passage of legislation that guaranteed racial equality under the law. The long-term goal was integration. That is, blacks would live alongside whites as complete equals in American society.

Malcolm X and the Nation of Islam rejected this vision. They preached that whites would never grant civil rights to blacks. "No sane black man really wants integration," Malcolm claimed. "No sane white man really believes that the white man ever will give

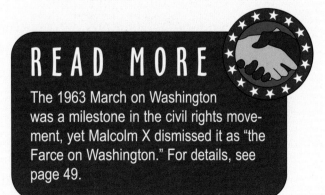

READ MORE

The 1963 March on Washington was a milestone in the civil rights movement, yet Malcolm X dismissed it as "the Farce on Washington." For details, see page 49.

Martin Luther King Jr. (left) and Malcolm X had vastly different views on how to win civil rights for African Americans, but by all accounts they respected each other. "Dr. King wants what I want," Malcolm once said. "Freedom." The two leaders met face-to-face only once, after a Senate debate on civil rights. This photo captured that brief meeting on April 26, 1964.

the black man anything more than token integration . . . the only solution is complete separation from the white man!"

If Malcolm X and the Nation of Islam disagreed with the goals of the mainstream civil rights movement, they also disagreed with its tactics. King was an advocate of civil disobedience. He believed that blacks should resist discriminatory laws and practices nonviolently, through such methods as protest marches, sit-ins at restaurants that served only whites, and boycotts of businesses or public transportation services that discriminated against African Americans. If civil rights protesters met with violence—and often they did—they were not supposed to strike back. This example of selfless devotion to the cause of justice, King believed, would ultimately appeal to the consciences of decent Americans.

Malcolm X, however, wasn't a believer in passive resistance. He didn't believe that whites—whom the Nation of Islam referred to as devils and snakes—could be swayed to do what was right. And he said that blacks should secure their rights by whatever means necessary, including violence.

Not surprisingly, many Americans found the Nation of Islam's message threatening. That feeling was reinforced with the July 1959 broadcast of a television documentary called *The Hate that Hate Produced*. It was narrated by veteran broadcaster Mike Wallace and featured interviews with Elijah Muhammad and Malcolm X. The Nation of Islam leaders were uncompromising in their condemnation of whites. The program led many viewers to conclude that hatred of whites was a core teaching of the Nation of Islam—and even that Black Muslims were plotting revenge against white America.

If many white Americans were alarmed, so too were many black Americans. They worried that the Nation of Islam's fiery rhetoric and militant stance threatened to reverse the progress that had been made in the area of civil rights.

Spotlight on Malcolm . . . and a Rift

The Hate that Hate Produced brought a new level of attention to the Nation of Islam. It also cast a spotlight on Malcolm X, who was besieged with interview requests. Malcolm gave countless speeches and lectured at universities. He refused to soften his tone, even when he was accused of hate mongering. "Why, when all of my ancestors are snake-bitten, and I'm snake-bitten, and I warn my children to avoid snakes, what does that snake sound like accusing me of hate-teaching," he wrote.

Malcolm had become the Nation of Islam's most prominent spokesperson. But quietly, behind the scenes, there was a rift developing between him and the Nation's other leaders. For

Malcolm always attracted a great deal of attention from reporters, but his comments on the assassination of President Kennedy ignited a firestorm of controversy.

years Malcolm had heard rumors that Elijah Muhammad had fathered a number of children with several of his secretaries, and he confirmed that the rumors were true. He was very upset that the head of the Nation of Islam, who publicly preached about the importance of upright behavior, was guilty of such moral lapses.

But there were other issues as well. By 1963, Elijah Muhammad was a sick man. Muhammad's children wanted to keep control of the Nation of Islam after their father's death. They saw Malcolm X, with his ability to stir audiences, as a potential threat to this plan.

Then, on November 22, 1963, President John F. Kennedy was assassinated. Americans were stunned. From the Nation of Islam's headquarters in Chicago, Elijah Muhammad issued a decree: no minister was to comment publicly on the assassination. In part this was out of respect for the feelings of the many African Americans who idolized the slain president. Kennedy had publicly championed the cause of racial equality.

Malcolm X, however, saw no reason to extol Kennedy's contributions or applaud the progress toward civil rights for African Americans. He would later write:

Four hundred years the white man has had his foot-long knife in the black man's back—and now the white man starts to wiggle the knife out, maybe six inches! The black man is supposed to be grateful. Why, if the white man jerked the knife out, it's still going to leave a scar.

Nine days after the Kennedy assassination, Malcolm delivered a speech at the Manhattan Center in New York. The title of the speech—which Malcolm had prepared before the assassination—was "God's Judgment on America." Malcolm was concerned about violating Elijah Muhammad's decree not to comment on Kennedy's killing. So he typed out the speech beforehand, which was unusual for him, and he stuck with the prepared text when he delivered the speech.

However, when Malcolm took questions after the speech and was asked about the assassination, he said that it was an instance of "the chickens coming home to roost"—meaning that the hatred and violence that whites had unleashed on blacks had returned to claim the life of the white American president.

Some members of the audience applauded. Others chuckled. But back in Chicago, no one at Nation of Islam headquarters was laughing. Elijah Muhammad prohibited Malcolm from speaking publicly for 90 days.

CHAPTER FIVE

FROM RAGE TO REASON

In early 1964, still shocked by Elijah Muhammad's order silencing him, Malcolm traveled to Miami with his family. He had been invited there by his friend Cassius Clay, a heavyweight boxer who was training for a title fight against the champion, Sonny Liston.

On the eve of the February 25 fight, Clay prayed with Malcolm for Allah's blessings. Clay was a huge underdog, but he stunned the boxing world by pummeling the champion. Liston was unable to answer the bell for round seven, making Clay the new world heavyweight champion.

Boxing fans—and the general public—soon got another big surprise. At a news conference the morning after he won the crown, Cassius Clay spoke about the Nation of Islam and defended Malcolm X. The following

Boxer Cassius Clay (center) with Malcolm X (left), Miami, Florida, February 1964. After defeating Sonny Liston to win the heavyweight title, Clay announced that he had joined the Nation of Islam and changed his name to Muhammad Ali.

day, the boxer announced that he had joined the Nation of Islam. He changed his name to Muhammad Ali.

Malcolm returned to New York to find himself embroiled in another controversy with the Nation of Islam's leadership. Malcolm had asked Elijah Muhammad directly about rumors of his affairs with secretaries. Muhammad had admitted that the rumors were true. Malcolm believed that it was just a matter of time before news of Muhammad's indiscretions became public. He thought this would discredit the Nation of Islam and demoralize members.

Malcolm searched the Bible and Quran for stories of great religious figures who'd had moral lapses. They included Noah, Moses, and David. Malcolm "began teaching in New York Mosque Seven that a man's accomplishments in his life outweighed his personal, human weaknesses." While his purpose was to prepare Nation of Islam members for the inevitable disclosure of Elijah Muhammad's sexual affairs, leaders in the Nation accused Malcolm of betraying Muhammad. From a former aide, Malcolm had even heard that a Nation of Islam official had ordered him killed.

Malcolm decided that the best thing to do was to make a complete break from the Nation of Islam. On March 8, he publicly announced that break. A few days later, he announced that he was forming a new group called Muslim Mosque, Inc. Though it was a religious organization, Muslim Mosque, Inc., would also seek to end the political, economic, and social oppression of America's 22 million black citizens, Malcolm said.

Malcolm's Hajj

In April, Malcolm began a journey that would change his life. He had decided to make the hajj—the religious pilgrimage to Mecca, which every devout Muslim is obliged to undertake, if possible,

Pilgrims on the hajj. Each year the pilgrimage draws 2 million to 3 million devout Muslims to Saudi Arabia.

at least once in his or her lifetime. Malcolm wanted to broaden his knowledge of Islam.

On the way to Saudi Arabia, Malcolm encountered Muslims who weren't black. "Packed on the plane," he recalled, "were white, black, brown, red and yellow people, blue eyes and blond hair, and my kinky red hair—all together, brothers. All honoring the same God, Allah, and in turn giving equal honor to each other."

READ MORE

For additional information about the hajj, Muslims' pilgrimage to Mecca, see page 50.

Malcolm experienced several harrowing days in the custody of Saudi officials when he landed in Jedda, Saudi Arabia. People who had converted to Islam in the United States were not welcome to make hajj, unless special authority was given by the Muslim high court.

Eventually, Malcolm got the permission he needed and made the pilgrimage, praying and chanting from sunrise to sunset for several days. He wrote home afterward, to his wife, family, friends, and professional acquaintances. The message was clear: the Muslim world was color-blind. Malcolm wrote:

> For the past week, I have been utterly speechless and spellbound by the graciousness I see displayed all around me by people of all colors. . . . What I have seen and experienced has forced me to . . . toss aside some of my previous conclusions . . . if white Americans could accept the Oneness of God, then perhaps, too, they could accept in reality the Oneness of Man—and cease to measure, and hinder, and harm others in terms of their "differences" in color.

After the Hajj

As is customary, Malcolm changed his name after his pilgrimage. He called himself El-Hajj Malik El-Shabazz.

For several weeks after the hajj had ended, Malcolm traveled throughout Africa. His reputation as a fighter for his American brothers, and his friendship with Muhammad Ali—whom Africans greatly admired—got him many invitations. He met with religious figures, government officials, scholars, and ambassadors.

Malcolm returned to the United States in May. He attracted a frenzy of media attention. Reporters wanted to ask about his views on race relations. Malcolm said that he no longer viewed whites as evil, and he no longer believed that blacks should live separately from whites. Still, he insisted that white American society remained racist, and he demanded that this change.

During the summer of 1964, simmering racial tensions erupted into race riots in a number of American cities. Many in

Police officers club an African American man in Harlem, 1964. Many members of the media blamed Malcolm X for racial violence during the summer of 1964.

the media wanted to blame Malcolm for the riots, because he insisted on the right of African Americans to defend themselves from attack. Unlike mainstream civil rights leaders such as Martin Luther King Jr., Malcolm refused to categorically renounce violence. "I am for violence," he said, "if non-violence means we continue postponing a solution to the American black man's problem—just to avoid violence. . . . I'm for violence exactly as you know the Irish, the Poles or Jews would be if they were flagrantly discriminated against."

New York police questioned Malcolm about his association with a rifle club in Harlem. The FBI also interviewed him.

Meanwhile, the Nation of Islam had filed a lawsuit to force Malcolm and his family out of their house in East Elmhurst, New York; the Nation had given the house to Malcolm before his rift with Elijah Muhammad. Worse, the feud between followers of the Nation of Islam and followers of Malcolm's Muslim Mosque, Inc., had turned violent. In late June of 1964, Malcolm wrote an open letter—which was printed in the *New York Post*—to Elijah Muhammad pleading for peace. "Instead of wasting all of this energy fighting each other," Malcolm wrote, "we should be working in unity and harmony with other leaders and organizations in an effort to solve the very serious problems facing all Afro-Americans."

Around the same time, Malcolm announced the formation of a non-religious organization that would promote black unity and human rights around the world. It was called the Organization of Afro-American Unity.

Malcolm also wanted the treatment of blacks in the United States brought before the United Nations. He wanted the UN to debate it as a human rights issue.

Borrowed Time

As 1964 came to an end, Malcolm remained at the center of controversy. Numerous people were watching him closely: the news media, New York police, the FBI and the CIA, angry representatives of the Nation of Islam. Given the climate of violence that prevailed, Malcolm knew that every day might be his last.

On the night of February 14, 1965, Malcolm, Betty, and their children were asleep in their home in East Elmhurst. Malcolm awoke to the sound of broken glass. He and Betty got up and saw that the living room was on fire. Everyone escaped unharmed, but the firebombing left Malcolm shaken.

Ella Little Collins, Malcolm's half sister, begged him to leave the United States for a few years. He could go to Africa and take one of the positions he'd been offered there, she suggested. "Everyone is walking around like zombies," Ella's son Rodnell wrote, "waiting for Dr. Death to knock on the door."

Death arrived one week later. On February 21, 1965, as Malcolm was getting ready to address a crowd at Manhattan's Audubon Ballroom, three gunmen rushed onto the stage and shot him at close range. He was pronounced dead on arrival at New York's Columbia Presbyterian Hospital. He was 39 years old.

In March 1966, three men were tried and convicted of first-degree murder in the killing of Malcolm X. Each was sentenced to life in prison. While all three were members of the Nation of Islam, it was never proved that they had acted on orders from the Nation's leaders.

Voice for Justice

During his lifetime, many people accused Malcolm X of being a hate monger and a racist. It was a charge he denied. "I am against every form of racism and segregation, every form of discrimination," Malcolm said. "I believe in human beings, and that all human beings should be respected as such, regardless of their color."

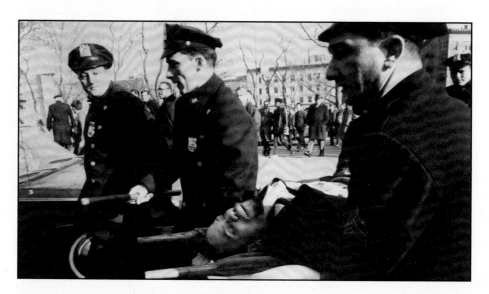

Policemen carry Malcolm X on a stretcher following his shooting, February 21, 1965. Malcolm was pronounced dead on arrival at the hospital.

There is no denying Malcolm's anger at the injustices committed against black Americans. That anger comes through clearly in his speeches and in his writings. But while Malcolm never publicly ruled out the use of violence to secure civil rights for African Americans, neither did he ever resort to committing violence or exhort his followers to do so. That fact was pointed out by the African American actor and civil rights activist Ossie Davis, who delivered a eulogy for Malcolm:

READ MORE

Movie director Spike Lee brought Malcolm X's life story to the screen in 1992. For details, see page 51.

> There are those who will consider it their duty, as friends of [black] people, to tell us to revile him, to flee, even from the presence of his memory, to save ourselves by writing him out of the history of our turbulent times. . . . They will say that he is of hate—a fanatic, a racist. . . . And we will answer and say unto them: Did you ever talk to Brother Malcolm? Did you ever really listen to him? Did he ever do a mean thing? Was he ever himself associated with violence or any public disturbance?

Malcolm believed that people who are oppressed cannot afford to be timid about claiming their rights. They must be willing to fight and sacrifice for justice. "You get freedom," he once remarked, "by letting your enemy know that you'll do anything to get your freedom; then you'll get it. It's the only way you'll get it."

Malcolm X's words, and his uncompromising commitment to justice for African Americans, continue to inspire more than 40 years after his death.

Norfolk Prison Colony

Malcolm described the Norfolk Prison Colony, which he entered in 1948, as too good to be true. Built during the 1930s, it was an experimental jail. The emphasis was not on punishing the prisoners, but on rehabilitating them so that they could leave as productive members of society.

Rather than living in cells, prisoners lived in dormitories. Each man had his own room. There were shower rooms, which the prisoners could use as often as they liked, as well as a ball field for those who wanted to exercise, and garden plots for those who liked growing their own food.

At Norfolk, the emphasis was on prisoner education. There were evening courses, in academic subjects as well as in subjects that would train the inmates for future jobs.

One of the most notable features at Norfolk was its library. Its large collection was donated to Massachusetts by Lewis Parkhurst, a state senator. Parkhurst had spent a big part of his career working for prison reform. Many of the books Malcolm read at Norfolk were a testament to Parkhurst's interest in religion and history.

An aerial view of the Norfolk Prison Colony.

Islam

Islam is one of the world's major religions, with more than a billion believers across the globe. Only Christianity has more followers.

Like Christians and Jews, Muslims—as followers of Islam are called—believe that there is only one God (or Allah). Muslims trace their lineage to the patriarch Abraham, a figure also revered by Jews and Christians. Muslims also accept as prophets many important figures from the Jewish and Christian traditions, including Adam, Isaac, Moses, and Jesus. But Muslims consider Allah's last and greatest prophet to be Muhammad.

Muhammad was an Arab born around A.D. 570 in Mecca, a city located in present-day Saudi Arabia. His parents died when he was young, and Muhammad was raised by his grandfather and then by his uncle. He grew up to be a respected trader and businessman.

Muslims believe that Muhammad was around 40 when he was first visited by the angel Gabriel, who relayed to him a message from Allah and ordered him to spread this message. Throughout the remainder of his life, Muhammad would periodically receive these messages from Allah. They are now recorded, Muslims believe, in Islam's holy scriptures, the Quran.

The essence of Islam is that believers must submit to the will of Allah. They demonstrate their commitment through the "five pillars" of Islam: *shahada*, a declaration of faith; *salat*, prayer five times each day; *zakat*, or the giving of money to charity; *sawm*, fasting during the holy month of Ramadan; and *hajj*, a pilgrimage to Mecca.

Marcus Garvey

One of 11 children, Marcus Garvey Jr. was born in 1887 on the island of Jamaica. As a young boy, he was apprenticed to a printer. He later got a position at a printing shop but was fired for his involvement in a labor union.

In 1910, Garvey left Jamaica and began traveling throughout Central America, where he worked as a newspaper editor. He learned through those early travels that many black people were living in poverty. In 1914, Garvey formed the Universal Negro Improvement Association (U.N.I.A). Its purpose was to encourage blacks to return to Africa, their ancestral home, and to form an independent nation there.

Garvey moved to the United States in 1916. He preached that the black race was superior to the white race. He also urged blacks to become financially independent of whites by starting their own businesses. Many black Americans were inspired by Garvey's message of self-respect. Others, however, were afraid that Garvey's views would only make trouble for them. They also didn't think it was realistic for them to return to Africa.

In 1923, Garvey was convicted of mail fraud. He eventually served several years in prison before being released and deported. He died in London in 1940.

Marcus Garvey encouraged blacks in the United States to return to their ancestral homeland of Africa.

The Allure of Harlem

Malcolm Little's main objective when he first arrived in Harlem was to have a good time. He was dazzled by the lights, the clubs, and the prosperous black people who enjoyed Harlem's nightlife.

Located in New York City's borough of Manhattan, Harlem was first settled by the Dutch in the 1600s. Small groups of black people were living in Harlem as early as 1880, primarily in rundown buildings called tenements. More blacks arrived after the turn of the century. Many came from the South. By the end of World War I in 1918, Harlem was an overwhelmingly black section.

During the 1920s, Harlem became arguably the most important center of black culture in the United States. Entertainment was a vital part of day-to-day life. In addition to the famous Apollo Theater and Savoy Ballroom, there were dozens of cafés, taverns, supper clubs, and dance halls throughout Harlem.

By the 1940s, Harlem's clubs and theaters had also become popular among whites. There, fans of jazz music could see the likes of Duke Ellington, Ella Fitzgerald, and Dinah Washington.

Lionel Hampton (right) leads his jazz band during a 1942 performance at Harlem's Savoy Ballroom.

The Significance of "X"

When he became a full member of the Nation of Islam, Malcolm dropped his "slave name" of Little and adopted the last name of "X." It was an important break with the life he had once led.

"X" represented the name and heritage that slaves lost when they were shipped to the United States. As slaves, blacks answered to whatever names their masters wanted to call them; they rarely had a last name. Common first names included Sambo, Prince, and Ben.

After the Civil War ended in 1865, freed slaves had to decide what to call themselves. Many took the last name of their former master. There were two reasons for this. First, most former slaves had no idea what their original names were. More important, because slaves were considered property—and were bought and sold at their masters' discretion—families were inevitably torn apart. Husbands were frequently separated from their wives, and children from their parents and siblings. In an effort to reunite with family members after the Civil War, many former slaves placed ads in newspapers. Using the last name of a former master afforded a better chance of success.

The March on Washington

On August 28, 1963, more than 200,000 supporters of civil rights—most of them African Americans—gathered on the National Mall in Washington, D.C. The event, dubbed the March on Washington for Jobs and Freedom, was organized by the leaders of six groups representing blacks. The goal was to put pressure on the Kennedy administration and the U.S. Congress to pass civil rights legislation.

One of the highlights of the March on Washington was Martin Luther King's famous "I Have a Dream" speech. From the steps of the Lincoln Memorial, King spelled out his vision of an America in which his "four little children will one day live in a nation where they will not be judged by the color of their skin but by the content of their character."

Many people believe that King's speech and the March on Washington were important factors leading to the passage of the Civil Rights Act of 1964, as well as the Voting Rights Act of 1965. These were major pieces of legislation promoting equality for black Americans.

At the time of the March on Washington, however, Malcolm X dismissed it as a big publicity event, dreamed up primarily by white people to make black Americans feel as if they were making progress. He sneeringly referred to it as "the Farce on Washington."

Civil rights supporters fill the National Mall during the March on Washington, August 28, 1963.

Making Hajj

If they are healthy enough and financially able, Muslims are expected to make hajj, the pilgrimage to Mecca in Saudi Arabia, at least once in their lifetime. Each year, some 2 million Muslims from around the world do so.

Hajj consists of several ceremonies, which symbolize the concepts of the Islamic faith and commemorate the trials of the prophet Abraham and his family. The pilgrimage takes place during the 12th month of the Islamic calendar, from the 8th to 12th days. Pilgrims can perform the rituals at other times of the year, but it is considered a "lesser pilgrimage" and does not fulfill the obligation for hajj.

Men and women can participate in hajj. Women usually wear a simple white dress. Men are required to wear two pieces of plain white cloth: one draped over the shoulder, the other covering their bodies from waist to ankle. The clothing is intended to show that everyone is equal in the eyes of Allah, whether they are a prince or a pauper.

While pilgrims are in this dress, they can't shave, clip their nails, or wear deodorant or perfume. They also can't quarrel, kill, or engage in sex.

Once hajj is completed, the pilgrim is considered free of sins.

Pilgrims on the hajj, Saudi Arabia.

Malcolm X, the Movie

The author Alex Haley began working with Malcolm X on his autobiography in 1963. It was published shortly after Malcolm's death in 1965, and it was the inspiration behind Spike Lee's movie of the same name, which was released in 1992.

The film featured actor Denzel Washington in the lead role. Washington spent an entire year preparing for the part. He cut down on alcohol, gave up pork (which is forbidden by Islam), read about Malcolm, and talk to people who knew him. Washington's performance drew excellent reviews from critics and earned him an Academy Award nomination for best actor.

Lee said that one of his main goals in making the film was to set the record straight about the life of Malcolm X, who had often been portrayed by the media as a fanatic revolutionary. Lee also wanted younger people to have a better idea about the spirit of Malcolm X.

The film closely follows Malcolm's autobiography. It covers Malcolm's life over three decades, showing his transformation from street punk to charismatic religious and political leader.

A scene from the 1992 film *Malcolm X*, featuring Spike Lee (left), and Denzel Washington (right).

Chronology

1925: Malcolm Little is born on May 19, in University Hospital, in Omaha, Nebraska.

1929: The Little home in Lansing, Michigan, is set on fire and burns to the ground on November 7.

1931: Malcolm's father, Earl, is run over by a streetcar and killed on September 28.

1939: Malcolm's mother, Louise Little, is committed to the state mental hospital in Kalamazoo, Michigan, on January 9, where she remains for 26 years. Malcolm is sent to a detention home run by the Swerlin family in Mason in August.

1940: Malcolm goes to Roxbury, Massachusetts, for the first time to visit his half sister Ella Little Collins.

1941: Malcolm moves to Roxbury to live with Ella in February. Over the succeeding months, he holds a variety of jobs and works on and off for the New Haven Railroad.

1943: Malcolm moves to Harlem in March and begins selling drugs, gambling, and stealing.

1946: Malcolm begins serving an 8- to 10-year prison term in Charlestown, Massachusetts, on February 27 for carrying firearms, larceny, and breaking and entering. He begins his own reading program.

1947: Malcolm is transferred to Concord Reformatory on January 10. He is introduced to the Nation of Islam and begins writing to Elijah Muhammad.

1948: Malcolm is transferred to Norfolk Prison Colony in March.

1952: Malcolm is released early from prison on August 7 after six and a half years behind bars. He personally meets Elijah Muhammad for the first time in September.

1953: In September, Malcolm becomes the first minister of the Nation of Islam's Temple Number Eleven in Boston.

1954: In March, Malcolm becomes acting minister of Temple Number Twelve in Philadelphia; in June he becomes minister of New York's Temple Number Seven.

1957: Malcolm founds the Nation of Islam newspaper, *Muhammad Speaks.*

1958: Malcolm marries Betty Sanders on January 14.

1959: Malcolm leaves for his first trip to Africa on July 5, where he will represent the Nation of Islam.

1963: On August 28, Malcolm attends the March on Washington as an observer; he is very critical of it. On December 4, he is suspended from the Nation of Islam and silenced by Elijah Muhammad for making controversial comments following the assassination of President John F. Kennedy.

1964: Malcolm officially breaks with the Nation of Islam on March 8. He founds Muslim Mosque, Inc. On April 19, he leaves for his pilgrimage to Mecca.

1965: Malcolm's home in East Elmhurst, New York, is firebombed on February 14. Malcolm is assassinated on February 21 after beginning to make a speech at the Audubon Ballroom in New York. He is buried at Ferncliff Cemetery in Hartsdale, New York, on February 27.

Further Reading

Blake, John. *Children of the Movement.* Chicago: Lawrence Hill Books, 2004.

George, Charles, editor. *Living Through the Civil Rights Movement.* Detroit: Greenhaven Press, 2007.

Goldman, Peter. *The Death and Life of Malcolm X.* 2nd edition. Chicago: University of Illinois Press, 1979.

Malcolm X. *Malcolm X Speaks.* George Breitman, ed. New York: Grove Press, 1994.

Rickford, Russell John. *Betty Shabazz: A Remarkable Story of Survival and Faith Before and After Malcolm X.* Naplewood, Ill.: Sourcebooks, 2003.

Tyner, James A. *Geography of Malcolm X: Black Radicalism and the Remaking of American Space.* London: Taylor & Francis, 2005.

Internet Resources

http://www.cmgww.com/historic/malcolm

Malcolm X's official site, run by his estate, includes a biography, facts, chronology of his life, and popular quotes.

http://www.brothermalcolm.net

This site contains scholarly research on Malcolm, his life, and activities.

http://www.colostate.edu/Orgs/MSA/find_more/m_x.html

Hosted by Colorado State University, this site details Malcolm X's conversion to Islam.

http://www.malcolm-x.org

This is a comprehensive site about the life and times of Malcolm X, including speeches, quotations, and some discussion of the Islamic religion.

http://www.columbia.edu/cu/ccbh/mxp/

The Malcolm X Project at Columbia University in New York is an ongoing effort to reconstruct the life of Malcolm X through multimedia resources and new historical research.

Glossary

autobiography—a book written about the true events of one's own life.

brainwashed—coerced or forced to adopt a certain set of beliefs.

civil disobedience—an organized refusal to obey laws in an effort to bring about social change through the use of nonviolent means.

civil rights—the nonpolitical rights of citizens, especially the rights associated with liberty.

Great Depression—a severe, worldwide economic crisis during the 1930s that left many people jobless and homeless.

Islam—the religion founded by the prophet Muhammad in the seventh century A.D.

hajj—a pilgrimage to Mecca in Saudi Arabia that all Muslims are required to make once in their lives, if they are healthy enough and have the financial means.

Harlem—a neighborhood in the New York City borough of Manhattan, long known as a thriving center of African American culture and business.

integration—the equal treatment and bringing together of people of different racial groups.

Muslim—a follower of Islam; characteristic of the religion, laws, and customs of Islam.

racism—hatred and intolerance of people of a different race.

Chapter Notes

Chapter 1: Freedom Behind Bars

p. 6 "He was the first . . ." Malcolm X with Alex Haley, *The Autobiography of Malcolm X* (New York: Ballantine Books, 1992), 79.

p. 8 "Months passed without . . ." Ibid., 203.

p. 8 "The ability to . . ." Ibid., 206.

p. 8 "world's most monstrous crime." Ibid., 189.

Chapter 2: Seeds of Hatred

p. 15 "snatched awake into . . ." Malcolm X, *Autobiography*, 5.

p. 15 "I remember we were outside . . ." Ibid., 6.

p. 16 "I just couldn't believe . . ." Ibid., 7.

p. 16 "Up you mighty . . ." Ibid.

p. 16 "Negroes in Lansing . . ." Ibid., 13.

p. 17 "They acted and looked . . ." Ibid., 16.

p. 18 "the first really proud . . ." Ibid., 39.

Chapter 3: Lessons from the Street

p. 21 "Malcolm, one of life's . . ." Malcolm X, *Autobiography*, 43.

p. 21 "All praise is due . . ." Ibid., 46.

p. 22 "despite our efforts . . ." Rodnell P. Collins, *Seventh Child: A Family Memoir of Malcolm X* (Secaucus, N.J.: Birch Lane Press, 1998), 40.

p. 23 "You know it's going to burn . . ." Malcolm X, *Autobiography*, 63.

p. 23 "You got a good conk." Ibid., 64.

p. 24 "I had always feared . . ." Ibid., 67.

Chapter 4: Growing a Nation

p. 31 "Betty was . . ." Malcolm X, *Autobiography*, 267.

p. 31 "No sane black man . . ." Ibid., 282.

p. 32 "Dr. King wants . . ." Quotes by Malcolm X. The Official Web Site of Malcolm X. http://www.cmgww.com/historic/malcolm/about/quotes_by.htm.

p. 33 "Why, when all my . . ." Ibid., 277.

p. 35 "Four hundred years . . ." Ibid., 311.

p. 35 "the chickens coming home . . ." Ibid., 329.

Chapter 5: From Rage to Reason

p. 37 "began teaching in New York . . ." Malcolm X, *Autobiography*, 326.

p. 38 "Packed on the plane . . ." Ibid., 373.

p. 39 "For the past week . . ." Ibid., 392.

p. 40 "I am for violence . . ." Ibid., 422.

p. 41 "Instead of wasting . . ." "Malcolm X Calls for Muslim Peace," *New York Times*, June 27, 1964. http://www.columbia.edu/cu/ccbh/mxp/images/source-book_img_131.jpg

p. 42 "Everyone is walking . . ." Collins, *Seventh Child*, 185.

p. 43 "I am against . . ." Quotes by Malcolm X. http://www.cmgww.com/historic/malcolm/about/quotes_by.htm.

p. 43 "There are those who . . ." Ossie Davis, eulogy for Malcolm X, delivered at Faith Temple Church of God, New York City, February 27, 1965. http://www.cmgww.com/historic/malcolm/about/eulogy.htm

p. 43 "You get freedom . . ." Cited in Adam Pachter, "Any Means Necessary," online guide to the PBS *American Experience* documentary *Malcolm X: Make It Plain.* http://www.pbs.org/wgbh/amex/malcolmx/sfeature/sf_means.html

Cross-Currents

p. 49 "four little children . . ." Martin Luther King Jr., "I Have a Dream" speech, August 28, 1963. http://www.americanrhetoric.com/speeches/mlkihaveadream.htm

Index

Numbers in **bold italics** refer to captions.

Photo Credits

About the Author

CAMMY S. BOURCIER is a writer and television producer who has worked on a wide range of projects—from pharmaceutical breakthroughs to Holocaust discoveries. She wrote "Shadows of the 70s," a 65-part series recapping that decade for the Associated Press, and has had more than 500 articles published on food trends.